# What Happens Is Neither

# What Happens Is Neither

Angela Narciso Torres

Four Way Books
Tribeca

*for*

*Carmen Tanseco Narciso*
13 September 1936 – 27 May 2019

*and*

*Francisco Villaruz Narciso*
2 October 1935 – 7 June 2019

Library of Congress Cataloging-in-Publication Data

Names: Torres, Angela Narciso, author.
Title: What happens is neither / Angela Narciso Torres.
Description: [New York] : [Four Way Books], [2021]
Identifiers: LCCN 2020037841 | ISBN 9781945588693 (trade paperback)
Subjects: LCGFT: Poetry.
Classification: LCC PS3620.O5894 W47 2021 | DDC 811/.6--dc23
LC record available at https://lccn.loc.gov/2020037841

This book is manufactured in the United States of America and printed on
acid-free paper.

Four Way Books is a not-for-profit literary press. We are grateful for the assistance
we receive from individual donors, public arts agencies, and private foundations.

This publication is made possible with public funds from the
National Endowment for the Arts

and from the New York State Council on the Arts, a state agency,

[clmp]

We are a proud member of the Community of Literary Magazines and Presses.

Contents

## If You Go to Bed Hungry

If you go to bed hungry, your soul will get up and steal cold rice from the pot.
Stop playing with fire before the moon rises or you'll pee in your sleep.

Sweeping the floor after dark sweeps wealth and good fortune out the door.
Fork dropped: a gentleman will visit. Spoon: a bashful lady.

Bathing after you've cooked over a hot stove makes the veins swell.
For safe passage to the guest who leaves mid-meal: turn your plate.

The adage goes: coffee stunts growth. Twelve grapes on New Year's: the opposite.
Advice from the learned: book under your pillow. Never step on. Never drop.

Every rice grain that remains on your plate you'll meet again on the footpath
to heaven. You'll have to stoop to pick up each one.

# Stone Fruit

Her sadness is coarse and thick as a horsehair coat.
As a child I tried it on. Its heavy folds engulfed me.

I learned to balance the weight on my head the way
fruit sellers carried baskets of mangoes on their crowns.

Mornings it cloyed to my throat like the hairy pits of drupes.
My eyes teared. I tried to spit. It insisted, impeded my breathing.

I swallowed the bitter stone. Washed it down like the whale
who gulped a grown man and kept him in darkness for days.

As a child I learned this from an aunt:
*If you swallow a seed, a tree will grow in your stomach.*

I nurture her sadness like a sapling.
Decades of summers pass. The tree fruits.

Lay your hand on my chest. Feel the heft
of sour-sweet drupes my mother's tears have fed.

# Sundowning

*for my mother, Carmen*

*The sweetest meat clings to the bone,*
my mother says, knifing her steak.
Carmen. Silver spade on my tongue.

Mahjong nights, her mother and father gone,
she cried herself to sleep. Blamed in the morning
for her mother's losing hand. *Unlucky tears!*

*The sweetest meat*—she begins at dinner,
tearing off a drumstick. What
will she recall by morning?

Named for Our Lady of Mount Carmel,
she pinned brown scapulars under our shirts,
wet stamps that cleaved to our backs.

Carmen. Prayer on the breath.
Amid potted ferns, she works
a jigsaw puzzle. Bizet on the radio.

Unable to sleep, she made me lie next to her.
My brothers clambered the banyan trees.
My legs twitched, a broken clock.

Her kisses are guava and rust. She sings
kundimans her mother sang.
*Sampaguita. Dahil Sa Iyo. Saan Ka Man.*

Sunday morning. Puzzle pieces
strewn on yesterday's news. Maria Callas
on the phonograph. Carmen.

Citrine fire. When she plays
the piano, the lovebirds fall silent.
Alabaster eggs tremble in glass bowls.

Afternoons, she woke with an urge
to bite the brown loaf of my arm.
The marks on my flesh faded by sundown.

*The sweetest meat clings—*
she insists. Peels a mango.
Amber rivers trace her elbows.

A trail of *L'air du Temps* wafts
in her wake. I follow it to her room,
dab the scent on my wrists and throat.

Evenings, she sang kundimans.
*Hatinggabi. Nasaan Ka Irog?* Carmen.
Song of the mangosteen moon.

*Before you go, I want to give you something.*
She hands me a thimble painted with a map
of Cuba. We've never been to Cuba.

In the dream, a sister pours rosary beads
into her cupped hands. Upon waking,
a dead wasp curled in her palm.

## Self-Portrait as Rosary Beads

Curled amid lint and loose change,
tucked in a jacket's satin lining or crushed
with used gum in seams of denim,
I've known pain clinics and airports, taxicabs
and stale schoolrooms where time is
a honeycomb in winter. I am olive wood,
carnelian, plastic, black onyx. Am rosebuds
pressed into fragrant spheres. Your heat,
is my musk; your worry, my fire. Pick
your mystery. If Tuesday: sorrowful, if Saturday:
glorious. I've held you in grocery lines,
picket lines, the hours between sleepless and
woken. Hold me. I am glass shattered, smoothed
by my mother's nerves, pillowed beneath
her cheek. Counted, accountable, counting,
counted on. Crystallized, dangled on a string
or hung from a mirror in a river of traffic,
praying for green, for an end, for a mutiny
of rain. Litany of sorrows, of praise,
I'm a crown of roses, a crown of purple
thorns. I am faithful as breadcrumbs
on barbed wire. Lose me to birds or to night's

starred thicket. Touch and be splintered,
sundered. Soothed, surrendered.
My scent on your fingertips.

## Recuerdo a mi Madre

I remember brownouts. Melted wax
cooling against my scar. How it
formed a pebbled lake bed.

Decades ago we spread blankets
on our parents' bedroom floor. I fell asleep
watching my beautiful mother sleep.

Cloaked in her frayed bathrobe, her guava
scent, I clutched my fears like lost teeth
then let them slip down the drain.

*

I've been avoiding the telephone,
spending dusty hours at the piano.

Broken chords. I stutter the cadenza.
Prolong the fermata. Each note

insists like the past.
Prayer and dirge.

\*

Today I let light have its way. Lavender
candles ribbon the air with scent.

Sun presses into a window.
Into silence a jackhammer drills.

I close my eyes
and see a trembling star.

\*

Finding my mother
crouched on the tiled floor,

her flickering eyes swollen,
the housedress she loved

in shreds, my father led us
outside. Called an ambulance.

Her silence an explosive
he'd learned to detonate.


*


My sister lights a trail
of ants with a match.

Some pop, others scurry
from a dead finch. A few linger,

stitching a loose border
around the bird's stone eye.

I couldn't look, couldn't
stop looking.


*


Bewildered, I grew up,
learned to embroider

an alphabet. I dipped my pen
in father's tears. To know

my mother requires
the patience of a miner

carving amethyst from rock.
To know my mother

is to memorize
a labyrinth of longing.

# Feather

The almost-neon sheen of moss
spreading like a stain on
the ash tree's grooved bark,

the hammock's frayed rope
to which the finches return,
trailing silk to their nests,

but mostly the quiet
of a neighbor's house, white
drapes billowing, bring back

those silences I moved in
as a child, a shadow slinking
through empty rooms.

Dust motes tunneled light above
the cold floor where, belly-down
I sprawled, goose feather in hand.

If I lay there long enough,
if I brushed the feather
on a fixed spot on the pebble-

washed floor, how long before
I'd make a dent? The point
is not that when night fell

there was barely a scratch. The point
is how, armed with a feather,
I believed I could make a mark.

## Kinds of Stillness

the egret leaning windward
  beak poised for stabbing
    shadows in the reeds

*

her eyes: milky panes
  between dream and confusion
    staring/not staring

*

as a child I thought
  sitting rock-still I could
    make time stop

*

the pen's nib hovers
  above the line      a hummer's
    electric wingbeats

*

the gap between tracks
  on a vinyl record—

# Disappearing Act

Mother chose the dress—mint-green with puffed sleeves. White starched collar, electric-pleat skirt, lace socks that chafed my ankles. At the party, she made me kiss everyone: aunts reeking of *Joy* by Jean Patou, swaybacked uncles cradling beers, my grandmother smoking clove cigarettes between puffs of her inhaler. Someone was laughing loudly. Someone played a ukulele. From a far table, the rumble of mah-jongg tiles being shuffled by a quorum of matrons, their lacquered nails clicking, wreathed in cigarette smoke. Cousins wrestled on the scorched lawn. A small place behind my ribs felt tender, making it hard to breathe. I wanted most of all to lie in the pink shell of my room, a book within reach. Someone passed around colorful sandwiches in the shape of card suits: diamonds, spades, clubs. Someone carried a tray of fizzy drinks, handing them to the grownups. I imagined sneaking a sip and getting smaller and smaller like Alice, then crawling into Mother's conch evening bag, the clasp closing overhead with a satisfied click. Mother whispered a greeting to a woman in a floral print kaftan. I vanished into their murmurs and shadows, a cloud of camphor and carnations.

## Ode to a *Realistic* AM/FM Radio
## at a Church Rummage Sale

What drew me was the rectangular squat of it,
the hefty boxful of sound you could plant

on a desk or shelf, its walnut veneer
nested among cables, chargers and string lights.

Next to me, a man inspecting a pair of headphones
saw me turn the radio over to check the tag

and smiled, more to himself than at me,
and I don't know why I told him

my dad had a radio just like it and, *isn't it cool,*
*those three silver dials and a lighted tuning*

*scale so you can see what station you're looking for?*
He picked up a scratched iPod before I could say,

*Look—no battery pack or carrying strap!* So when
your mother settles down to her talk show,

she's bound to stay where she is, paying bills
or reading or filing her nails, just like my dad

when he turned on his shiny Panasonic, permanently
set at DZFX *contemporary sound of radio in Makati*

while he signed papers or typed on the Smith Corona
as I sprawled on the rug, knowing he'd stay

riveted until Beethoven's Symphony No. 7,
performed by the Vienna Philharmonic Orchestra

and conducted by Karl Böhm, reached its grand finale.
But for now the first movement was just gaining momentum.

It would be a while before the tsunami of brass
and strings that broke through the staticky silence would end

in applause and we'd stand up to do the routine
things around the house—but not yet—

not while that spell of sound held us,
pouring from a silver box rooted to the wall

and my father, leaning back in his chair,
eyes fixed in the middle distance between desk

and darkening window, wasn't going anywhere,
and the brown shag rug beneath us wasn't going anywhere.

## Prelude and Fugue

Something of late November
  sifting through a window
brings back this prelude.

  Two voices blend, I lean
into the keys, draw back
  when the voices part.

How the body remembers—
  Señora V. in a floral dress,
talcumed hand soft

on the curve of my spine
  imprinting what she knew
of love and time. How could I know

  what those notes would mean
decades of preludes ahead.

## Alzheimer's


there was a piano she loved

        *cherubs carved on cherry wood*

hands ripple over ghost keys

        she nods off, chin to chest

*do you want to lie down?*      *no*

        under the palms in a pink housedress

*what is your name?*      she asks

        again      *cherubs playing violins*

sunlight slips behind ferns

# Lines from a Journal I

*a cento using lines from Katherine Mansfield's journal*

The year is nearly over.
A thick white mist reaches the edge of the field.
There is no limit to human suffering.
I am sad tonight. Perhaps it is the wind.


A thick white mist reaches the edge of the field.
This joy of being alone. What is it?
I am sad tonight. Perhaps it is the wind.
The black chair, half in shadow, as if a happy person sprawled there.


This joy of being alone. What is it?
I feel the new life coming nearer.
The black chair, half in shadow, as if a happy person sprawled there.
For all the sun, it is raining outside.


I feel the new life coming nearer.
And then the dream is over and I begin working again.
For all the sun, it is raining outside.
I feel always trembling on the brink of poetry.


And then the dream is over and I begin working again.
Am I less of a writer than I used to be?
I feel always trembling on the brink of poetry.
Sometimes I glance up at the clock.

Am I less of a writer than I used to be?
I must begin all over again.
Sometimes I glance up at the clock.
To look up through the trees to the faraway blue.

I must begin all over again.
To live—to live—that is all.
To look up through the trees to the faraway blue.
I want to remember how the light fades from a room.

To live—to live—that is all.
There is no limit to human suffering.
I want to remember how the light fades from a room.
The year is nearly over.

# Pearl Diving

*Is Memory, / as they pretend, / mother of the Muse?— /
or Forgetting,*
—James Richardson

1/


She lapses into music, rising from dinner to play piano as we eat and
talk. As if togetherness were a storm cloud in June, filled to bursting.
A brooding monsoon.


2/


Her memories, black pigeons flying off at dusk. Who knows where
they spend the night? Dawn finds them back at the cote, softly
cooing. In time their flights will cover greater distances. Some will
disappear for days. A few will never return.


3/


When my father comes home from work, she claps like a birthday
child: *Papa!* A pause. *Where's my husband?* My father, swallowing
hard. *Still at work, hija.*


4/


Casting my line in a dark pool, I bait her memory like fish. *Mother,
who painted that portrait of you? Tell me your lola's recipe for oxtail*

*stew. When did you learn to play the kundimans?* Her eyes, two searchlights, sweeping.

5/

Later in bed she turns to him. *Where's Kit, Papa?* He dresses in darkness, retrieves his violin case from the hallway. *I'm home,* he says, kissing her forehead. He sits on her side of the bed till she falls asleep.

6/

Have you heard of the pearl divers of Davao—mere boys plowing headfirst into the freezing deep, holding their breaths for minutes at a time to find the largest oysters, the ones that might hold the prized black pearl, their only light—dim lamps tied to their foreheads?

7/

Her lips form the words to the Our Father all the way to the Great Amen. Her fingertips roll invisible rosary beads.

8/

My father's voice cracks over the phone. She's been looking for you, he says. Calls you *Mama* or *Sister Amelita.* Or sometimes, *that little girl who was just sitting there.* I've been playing kundimans for her, he says. She knows the words.

# Confessions of a Transplant

My first year living in America
the scent of frying garlic
sent me weeping. My eyes

swept the somber avenues,
starving for color. I devoured
the aquamarine of broken glass,

a wire festooned with yellow shoes,
the shower of plum blossoms
on a sidewalk. The memory

of sour mangoes made rivers
in my mouth. At the market, I picked
the greenest nectarines, dredged them

in salt that stung my chapped lips.
Words I hoarded like rock
candy, melted on my tongue

like my too-hard r's. *Range Rover, red*
*robin, river rock.* I practiced
into the ear of an empty flagon,

reciting litanies to the saint
of lost things. The walls
echoed with whispers.

Lying lily-still in the goblet
of night, I drank the croons
of nameless birds.

## Translating the Dead

two days after grandfather died
his letter arrived from Manila
sky blue aerogramme
trifolded and sealed
by the aunt who kept vigil
typing for him what words
he had left on the Smith Corona
with the broken lowercase *i*
that pierced holes through paper
I remember school nights
finding him still
awake listening
for my backpack's thud
on the wood floor
leading to his bedroom
slowly he'd rise
a smoker's cough
clearing his throat
his voice tunneling
in half-dark
*Are you here now, hija?*
a direct translation
from Tagalog
*Nariyan ka na, anak?*

meaning *You're here, child?*
meaning *I've been waiting, dear one*
holding the crinkled sheet
against the October sky
I find another sky
deeper blue
pinpricks of light
shining like Day-Glo stars
*Yes, Papa. I'm here.*

# Slash-and-burn

Cut grass thickens. Deadheaded
gardenias flower furiously.
Uprooted weeds regrow. Faster.

Years after, the babysitter confessed
she clipped my baby brother's lashes
with a nail trimmer. *To make them long,*

she said sweetly. Pushed back,
cuticles return tougher, thicker.
Shave your head, grow a forest.

At twelve, I wanted a razor
for the fine hairs on my legs. *Don't—*
my mother said. *They'll grow back*

*coarse, then you'll be shaving every day.*
When I jumped to take a boyfriend's
call, my sister pinned me down. *Make him*

*wait. Be expensive*—my grandmother
added. *Grow scarce and he'll spill*
*orchids at your feet.* Like the lushness

of undergrowth after slash-and-burn.
The extravagance of a scar
after insult to the flesh.

# Concha

I remember nights in that arid town—
boxes half-unpacked, back door

cracked to desert wind, frat boys'
thick laughter from a window.

Bonnie Raitt on autorcpeat: *I can't*
*make you love me, if you don't—*

convincing me her pain was mine.
In the darkness, wailing. *Peacocks,*

the landlady smiled. I remember my first
day at the agency, a new diploma framed

above my metal desk. I arranged
paperclips for hours in my fitted suit

and sensible heels. Across the hall,
Don in his bolo tie, chair tipped back,

lizard-skin boot crossed over knee,
phone cradled in the crook of his neck.

Cigarette smoke coiled from a slit
in his door. My caseload: seven green

folders, seven children needing homes,
seven knots in my stomach not unlike—

but not quite—Christmas Eve. How,
before reading the files, I walked

to Estrella's for coffee and a pink-
sugared concha. How I found, back
E
at my desk, a single condom in its foil,
squared neatly on the stacked folders.

Driving home, dusk's fingers slid over
sleeping adobe houses and saguaros

thrust their stout limbs to the sky.
My landlord's night-blooming

cereus opened its tiny mouths
but offered no words.

# The Immigrant Visits Her Mother

Those tropical mornings I woke to no sun
in a shuttered room, the shuffle of slippers
at my door, hall light flooding the gap
her slight frame could not fill, smaller
than when I last saw her. Through the net
of sleep floated her voice, repeating
my name. I rose, stumbled to my feet,
offered my arm. Her good leg leading,
we made our way to the dim-lit table
where I sliced a bagel neatly in half,
fed it to the glowing toaster. When the rounds
popped out—fragrant, golden—
I spread the cream thin with a knife,
layered the slivers of smoked salmon
from the packet I'd carried from Chicago,
a twist of lemon to finish. One bite
and her eyes glazed over, forehead
uncreased. For a moment she was
twenty-six, a medical student again,
lipsticked and bone-tired from her shift
sitting at a Brooklyn diner to coffee,
a bagel, and the *Times*. Here, decades
and hemispheres away, dawn burns
through Manila smog, licks the blinds

of the kitchen where my mother fills
her mouth with the salt and sting
of her first New York winter
the year before I was born.

## Warm Spell, February

For the first time in weeks the wind doesn't cut like an insult.
My dog feels it too. I slacken her leash so she can dig her nose

in the wet underbrush, letting her sniff as long as she likes.
A woman walking on a San Francisco beach once told me,

*We need to give them time*—meaning the dog, snout-deep in tangled
seaweed. *To them, it's like reading a very good book.* Somewhere I read

Haruki Murakami trained for marathons the way he writes—
pushing his legs to the next mile like he pushed his pen to the end

of one sentence, and then the next. Today I'm in no rush. I tread
slowly, sipping the air the way the Pacific Ocean swallowed

our brown bodies just outside Manila, our mothers
waving us back to steamed rice, fried fish, mango on a stick.

Why do I remember? Would I think of this now if the air weren't
soft with last night's showers, warm as a mother's breast? Would I dare

to say, *the twigs are chandeliered with rain like pearls from a girl's ear?*
I breathe. For the first time in weeks I'm returned to my skin.

# Pont des Arts

Near the bridge's end, the cripple
hobbled to a stop, an empty can
outstretched in his gloved hand.

By the time we dropped a few coins
and reached the other side, the sky
had turned black, a dense fog

swallowing the barge's cries. Our last
night in Paris and we were ready
for discord. Was it the wine,

the want of sleep, the relentless feast
of beauty? When I fell silent at the Jardin
des Plantes, your eyes stayed fixed

on the fountain. I slowed my pace
at Varenne station; you thought I'd lost
an earring. Back at the hotel I sobbed

in the shower, you flipped through channels
though all of them were in French.
Combing my wet hair, I pictured the steps

of Saint-Sulpice, carved by centuries
of heels pounding toward salvation.
Does anyone believe the world was made

for happiness? That night we crossed
the Pont des Arts under a plum sky,
padlocks winking like tumbled stars

trapped in the guardrails, the tossed
keys rusting the river.
Is it human or animal—this urge

to bind and tear apart,
to pick at old scabs and howl
from our softest parts?

# September, Chicago

*a Golden Shovel using a line from Gwendolyn Brooks*

Almost metallic—this bite in the air—even
    if the almanac says eleven days till autumn. But the
birch trees are impossibly green and the only leaves

turning are these blue-lined pages. Windblown, they fall
    open to where I erased your name. Down,
down to the basement went your letters, still bound in

June heat. Was your handwriting always lovelier
    under a bare bulb? The light bleeds patterns
through ink & paper, insistent glyphs that spell, *Wait. Still here.*

## Repainting the House

All day, from every wall, the sound of scraping.
Painters on ladders strip the chipped white
siding on this old house. There's no escaping
orbit sander, rasp, and putty knife.
Their tools, like locusts, peel the tattered layers
that drift like early snow, the wood's deep
grain exposed. Autumn chills the air,
they rush to fill the cracks before rain seeps
and soaks good cedar into rot. Inside, I turn
the radio on. Some tune about regret.
A line brings back the time I learned
you'd gone.
                What the heart forgets.
Later, through white-flecked grass I draw the rake—
cicada husks beneath the fallen flakes.

# Shed

It was something we always watched for
but never saw—the gecko unsheathing
her transparent full-body tunic,
each wrinkle and bump intact, a record
of growth like the rings in a tree. Eight
years on a ledge by our kitchen window,
slinking in a clear box furnished
with egg cartons and yogurt cups
and never once did we catch her
in the act. It was almost always
morning when we'd find the discarded
sheath in a corner of the tank—a crumpled
shadow, like the satin slip a woman steps from
in haste, rippling on the floor,
still warm with her scent.

## Narrow Bed

Carpenter ants picked the T-bone clean.

The dog's leash tautened toward

a square of sun.

A hallway lamp wavered.

Slice of lit motes through

the cracked bedroom door.

Her slipper under the bed, another on the armoire.

On the shell comb, a single strand.

Her chenille robe still damp.

*

a narrow bed in an endless
row of beds tucked tight
like chalk-white pills
cocooned in plastic

no visitors no cellphone no
end to night but the nurse
who relayed messages
telegraphic—send purple

bathrobe Saint Jude
rosary lime-flavored
Jell-O bedroom slippers
boar bristle brush

*

*why am I here?*

pressed in her suitcase
between terrycloth and silk


*where is my husband?*

on a prescription slip, scribbled
in her physician scrawl


*when will I go home?*

barely three days before
the words slowed to a trickle

# At Lula's


Because the sun feels like medicine
when they leave the café
they stop at a park bench, resuming

those stories between friends
like a piece of knitting—with neither
beginning nor end. Hair billowing,

they gather their losses
into brief bouquets.
Some petals break loose.

## To the One We Lost

child      when the blue-black sac of you      dropped

     a yolk of matted cells      and plasma      into the toilet's

bone-white walls      i blamed the rain      the fried eggplant

     the trip to the mall      blamed my past selfish ways

faulted the oak      that fell across      our fence

     while you      sailed off      my second      my spawn

little prawn      i never met      peaceful

     you floated      from your watery cave

to the salty grottos      of the sea

     where perhaps      a spiny anemone      caught you

in its tentacles      a coral bed      your cradle

     and the manatee moaned      a mournful song

# Ode to the Areola

Dark pigmented nebula
deepening around the nipple
after childbirth, purple
haze surrounding
the storm's eye

not to be confused with
*aureole*—that crown of light
radiating from saints' heads
in certain Medieval paintings
from the Latin *aureolas*
derived from *aurum*
meaning, "gold"

which is also the root for *oriole*—
those amber-plumed passerines
flashing against July's late foliage
aging from Kool-Aid lime
to hunter green. Until recently

I thought *areola* descended
from the same root for orioles
and saint's crowns. But in fact
it derives from the Latin word

for "open place"—which might
connote a sun-filled plaza
somewhere in Tuscany

and not a chocolate cloud
capping the snowy flesh
my newborn rooted for at dawn
his mouth a wrinkled rose.

# The Foul Rag and Bone Shop of the Heart

*a Golden Shovel using a line from William Butler Yeats*

I'm not just talking about the
sleepless days and nights, the nonstop nursing, the foul-
smelling diapers. I'm talking of how my body reeked, a soaked rag
of curdled milk, drool, and leaky nappies; &
how I'd wake already beat beyond blood, bone
& breath, the babe still at my breast. But when I pushed past a shop-
window the other day, I turned to do a double-take: a glimmer of
a woman I once knew. No, it wasn't just the
wind-tossed hair, the morning-weary face. But oh, the heart, the heart!

# Return

Eucalyptus trees root where we left them,
lining the road that winds to the house
where our sons were born. Trunks
twist skyward like Michelangelo's
marble gods. Fewer evergreens, more
parking garages than I recall. Our Lady
of Peace has lost her sheen and heft.
Past the creek, in the vacant lot
where our boys rode their bikes
to hunt peeper frogs in spring
a stadium has bloomed overnight.
Floodlights shine like foil against
the blackened sky as we drive past,
throwing long shadows on the sidewalk
whose edges still bear the scars
from my son's skateboard.

# After Dinner at Fisherman's Wharf

Beyond Old Fisherman's Grotto
the sea lions bark, turning mournfully
in the inky harbor. The lights
have gone out at Carousel Candy

but the gears keep cranking
behind the window, stretching
and pulling pink taffy
into the night. Spent,

a young father cradles his sleeping
infant in a sling. Sun-sick toddlers
drop their sweaty heads like October's
last dahlias. Scores of seasons past,

our boys ran circles on this deck,
planets in orbit. Tonight we hold only
each other as we cross the briny planks.
Above, the clouds are heavy with blessed rain.

## Self-Portrait as Water

*why does the body feel*
    *more beautiful underwater—*
is what goes through me

    when I break the glass
surface, levels rising as I plumb
    the tub's white womb

this second skin thinner,
    slicker, gleaming wet
as a lacquered bowl

    because the simplest
of molecules—two H's
    one O—love

to love each other, cling
    to what they touch
how this universal solvent

    swallows every hill
fills the hollows
    of my surrender

most forgiving of
        substances, I resolve
to live like you—to fill

        and be filled,
to take the shape
        of my vessel

dispensing heat
        displacing matter
lighter than air

# Four Years after Diagnosis

Sudden rain. Our heads
  bowed together like monks
in this hot green place.

  I study the slow script
of her movements. The cross
  and uncross of her legs,

fingers forking together,
  pulling apart. Secret dialect
of her face: a firefly flick

  in the iris, lips curling
like kelp. Speak, mother.
  Your daughter is listening.

# Relief Map

Awake at 2 a.m., my gut twists
with a pang it cannot name. Earlier,
a beeline of ducks on the parking lot,
one struck by a car, still flailing.

How the mother flapped, hovered—
refusing to cross to safety. Standing
with a poet by the festival tent, noon heat
baking my scalp, he asked what scent I wore,

remarked how sweet. A friend writes
of the blistering loneliness of midlife,
this textbook mother, this ideal wife whose
marriage was a rock. Does sadness bind

or divide? And what of desire that seizes
my breath while he sleeps—his own breath
slow and steady? Tolstoy called boredom
the desire for desires. It is June

when I revisit my college, halfway across
the globe. Along the cobbled path,
flame trees touch their torched
fingers to the breeze, branches hung

with silk strands bearing dozens of pupae.
In four days they'll turn into giant moths.
But first, the wind must cause a single
worm to brush its hairy body

against my arm. Welts will rise on the wrist,
islands on a map, raw and flushed as my face
where my mother struck me once, leaving
a sting no known balm could salve.

# To Replace a Tree Eaten by Ash Borers Requires a New Vocabulary

City workers plant a green
sapling labeled *autumn*
on the sidewalk. Resistant
to leaf-scorch, they say. Seven
Midwestern winters and I'm
pale as a stripped birch.
I've stopped using *splendor*
to describe what happens
in spring. Body, my bark—
my first, my last. How
*horse* is only one letter
away from house. Once,
my grandfather called me
*chestnut* for the caramel-
brown skin I was born in.
While my sister pinked
liked a steamed shrimp,
I roasted, never peeled.
Where are the unanimous
trees of June?

# August

Something in this garden
is dying. Last week's
poppies have gone to seed

and today the honeysuckle dries
on the branch. Every day one
day closer—maybe somebody

else, maybe you—or me.
Another ash tree
taken down. This is

nothing new.
My father's cancer
has spread—tiny maps

colonizing his spine.
How or where to keep
this slow-growing grief?

All these small
departures—
and large, islands

on the horizon,
green dark mysteries
I cannot know.

## Nocturne

Awake beneath an onyx sky you crack the blinds, inhale
night's fading ink. The air is your mother's breath on your skin,
the only steeple is the church of palms in the neighbor's yard

dropping vermilion fruit on the grass. On another coast,
everyone you know is sleeping except for a boy you love.
In his body ticks a clock that matches yours. Darkness seeps

from blades of palmetto the way water leaves your fingers
after a bath. To see the darkness, one must look darkly. Hours later,
this boy will feed his cat, perform his daily ministrations

like a mother. What is parenting but a prayer for one's young.
Outside, the white ibis of dawn unfurls the potted mint,
its ribbons of scent. Son, your shadow lives in my eyes.

# Some Uses of Friction

A hazelnut's husk is thinnest paper.
Rubbing the roasted globes between
my palms, I make brown rain.
In my hand: five dusty suns.

When mother's memory became a slide
I planted questions like sandpaper. *Isn't*
*that so-and-so*—in the frame at her bedside.
Some things caught. Others didn't.

Crickets have teeth on their bottom wing.
The upper wing brushes across the teeth
to make sweet music. And flies?
They rub their legs to keep them clean.

When we had to decide if she should move
to a home, two camps formed: a silent war.
We'd been warned: *A parent's illness could*
*cause friction.* The very air rubbed us raw.

Dry grass wedged in ancient rock.
A hunter picks up a stone,
takes aim, strikes the rock.
And the first sparks fly.

# Watch

Here in these cracked
walls of mortar and wood,
of mother's daily erasures
and father's thinning
wrists—here in this
reluctant drawer

rests my father's watch
its gold weave band
gone from amber to
dun, the latch empurpled
to iridescent plum. The time

is always 5:17, the second
hand still at forty-two,
the face's tiny window declares
Thursday the twenty-first
of some long buried month.

Why the *second* hand and not
the third? By what magic
did minutes keep ticking
by a few shakes of his wrist
as though he were playing

maracas, solemn-faced, while
my mother put on makeup? What
made the dots, one for each hour,
the hands that moved with the sun
glow green in the dark?
Why that day, that minute,

that second? The mute face stares
through years of scruff and grime.
My father dozes in his chair.
A symphony lingers to its close,
his wrinkled hand beating time.

## What Isn't There

Even without leaves
the Bradford pear keeps
its bell silhouette.

Above, a commonplace moon,
somewhere between half
and full, waxing edge

rubbed like the worn
ridges of a lucky quarter.
A sentence partly

erased—brightness
that might have been.

## Suburban Backyard in Late July

Black-eyed Susan, coneflower, China rose—
all that remains when I return, blooming
without irony in my spent garden.
When I left my mother it was monsoon season,
the strongest typhoon to hit the islands
in years. Thirty villages buried in mud.
How could I know, two months later,
that she'd awaken in a white room
in a white gown, a plastic wristband
the only reminder of her name?
Mother's eyes appear from the deep—
one minute glazed, the next,
burning holes through a window,
listening for footfall. Who is this
woman without her nocturnes,
painted saints crowding her nightstand,
the mute phone winking day and night?
Whose face, unframed by kohl
and rouge, no crimson lips
pouting at the mirror
to bear her into the day?
I deadhead the salvias,
bring them to water.

# Lines Borrowed from a Marriage and Other Places

When asked how she could make her orchids bloom,
the gardener said, go inside and read a good, thick book.

At the groomer's, several people fawned over her dog.
One of the staff members hung back. The dog barked

repeatedly until she got his attention. *I never
change, I simply become more myself.*

On a shelf in her son's apartment, she found
her dog-eared copy of Frost's *Poems*. She took it

from the shelf; it fell open to a pasture.
*"I shan't be gone long.—You come too."*

Nights, she listened to Bach's Goldberg Variations.
It's not that it made her instantly happy; it turned

her sadness into something she recognized. *Today
again I am hardly myself. It happens over and over.*

At the kitchen store, she found the beechwood
mixing spoon, smooth and white, a wedding gift

they misplaced in the move. When she showed him,
he said, why didn't you buy the silicone kind?

*I've already lost touch with a couple of people I used to be.*
Despite neglect, the lavender thrives in its plastic pot.

# The Abscission Layer

*a semi-found poem from an Encyclopedia Britannica*
*article on leaf anatomy*

abscission layers form when leaves

    *know when it's time to go    as apples*

are damaged by insects, disease, drought

    *sometimes hearts cannot recoup*

their normal formation in autumn

    *like one cracked open or*

appears to be, in part at least

    *when the blues descend*

due to the shortening of the day

    *come autumn*

perhaps the shorter days accentuate

    *a lack of dopamine in the brain*

the senile changes normal in older leaves

*making everything look bleak*

*the jagged calligraphy of twigs*

*I can barely lift my head*

*{infusion of ginseng and bergamot}*

*I breathe    watch for color*

*I look for signs of budding*

as a result, a zone of cells across

the petiole becomes softened until

the leaf falls    a healing layer

salves the stem and closes the wound

leaving the leaf scar—a prominent feature

in many winter twigs

73

## What Happens Is Neither

the end nor the beginning.
Yet we're wired to look for signs.
Consider the peonies. One makes
a perfect bud after months of nothing.
Another's leaves are ringed with
black rot. How can I not think, *end*.
How can I not say, *beginning*.

Leaves fall when days shorten
because a tree must reduce
to its tough parts—twig, branch,
bark. My mother sleeps away
the daylight. She nods off while
chewing a spoonful of fish and rice,
her head a peony gone to seed.

Father calls to say she doesn't
recognize him. Turning to him,
she cried out, certain a stranger
was in her bed. He played
his violin till she slept—a leaf
in late fall curling into itself.

In autumn, chlorophyll disappears,
cancelling green from leaves
so yellow and magenta can blaze.
In my mirror I see her—the smile
that favors a cheek, eyes slanting
in the shape of small fish
we eat for breakfast.

Trees know best the now of things.
What goes on has been going on
for centuries. Washing dishes, I rest
a foot on my standing leg. A fork clangs
on the tile. I rinse a cracked cup.
I try not to think of endings.

## Lilli's Urn

Jolted awake by a flash—
a text from my college freshman
awake in his dorm at 2 a.m.

I rub sleep from my eyes,
find an audio clip
he's written for solo cello—

Lilli's Urn, he names it,
for the pup who arrived
on his sixth birthday,

his companion for a decade
before we lost her to cancer.
Four minor notes plucked

in a slow chuffing beat—
the stifled sobs of mourning.
Bow dragged over strings

the cello moans, whale
sounds from the deep. Outside,
the wet boughs of a birch

cradle a quarter moon. Rain
silvers branch tips, pavement,
the whole weeping world.

## The Morning I Hear

the word *metastasis*, colonies of rogue
cells occupying my father's spinal cord,
I pick a peach from the chipped bowl,
cup its weight in my palm. I slit

one end, rocking the knife's handle
till blade meets stone. The halves split
exposing the wooden pit. I slice eight
wedges, arrange them on a plate.

The slice I choose is crimson-pocked
as though it were touched by
the princess who pricked her finger
and slept a hundred years.

More tang than sweet, it sends
a twinge to my ear. Blinking back
tears, I scrape my teeth against the pit
and eat: grit, flesh—and all.

# Breathe

*find that place between effort*
*and ease,* the voice says

we double over like caterpillars
folding our bodies into

not-so-perfect halves
torsos trying to simulate

wet rags over rods
arms hover limp

and all I feel is
the tug of pain

tracing hamstrings
and this urge to steal

a sip of water
just out of reach

like the place between
effort and ease

## Reading This Poem at My Father's Funeral I Choke on the Word "Balsamic"

Sundays he took me along on his errands,
Mother on her midday siesta, Sister in bed
with the crossword. The afternoon was ours.
Keys jangling in his free hand, my fingers wrapped

in his other, we'd cross the concrete parking lot,
three of my steps to each of his long strides.
It's all business, his face read, but from his grip
and the way his shoulders lurched forward,

I knew the day held more. At the camera shop
Anna smiled behind the shiny counter,
handing him the sealed Kodak packets
of photographs from a family vacation. Once

we bought rabbit ears at the hardware, metallic
smells of commerce assaulting our senses.
In the store he'd study Mother's list, her slanted
script almost touching his thick glasses.

He picked balsamic vinegar when the recipe called
for white, Superman Band-Aids, rocky road ice cream.
In the stationery section he lingered, drawn by the scent
of pencils, fresh reams of paper, rubber bands

by the hundreds. I remembered his stories of the war,
how his mother hoarded paper in every form—brown bags
folded and refolded, moth-eaten receipts, calendars,
the gray-white margins of newsprint on which he practiced

his letters as a boy. The last item checked and bagged,
we headed for the exit, arrested by garlic peanuts
and Mang Tony's toothy grin. We held out paper cones,
he filled them to the brim, greasy parchment warming

our palms. Years ahead, when a trip to the store became
a mere stop in a blur of chores, I'd remember stepping
off the sidewalk with my father, our cart freewheeling,
bundles coming loose in the vast afternoon.

# Chore

My friend turns anything into
prayer. Sweeping the leaves, shaving
his beard, washing dishes—

every act a purging
of what doesn't serve. Today
I'm folding laundry. I start with jeans,

crisp from the dryer, smoothing the creases
then draping them on wooden hangers.
Shaking wrinkles from the sheets, I square

the corners the way Mother taught.
White T-shirts stacked flat on a shelf,
sundresses on felt hangers, sweaters

nestled in drawers. I find a place
for every blouse, every scarf, until
it feels inevitable. *Order our days*—

the remnant floats up from decades
of Sundays like words of a forgotten
song—*in Your peace.* My mantra:

*fold, hang, repeat,* the hamper
half-empty, the bureau warm
with balled up socks.

# Lines from a Journal II

*a cento using lines from Virginia Woolf's diaries*

Truth is, one can't write about the soul. Looked at, it vanishes.
Why have I so little control?
One wants to finish sentences.
To go adventuring on the streams of other people's lives.

Why have I so little control?
This is the normal feeling, I think.
To go adventuring on the streams of other people's lives.
I take a census of happy people, and unhappy.

This is the normal feeling, I think.
Happiness is a little string onto which things will attach.
I take a census of happy people, and unhappy.
How Vita's inkpot flowered on her table.

Happiness is a little string onto which things will attach.
How can I express the darkness?
How Vita's inkpot flowered on her table?
Shall I remember any of this?

How can I express the darkness?
At this moment, all we wish is to escape seeing.
Shall I remember any of this?
I am repeating things.

At this moment, all we wish is to escape seeing.
The world swinging round again, bringing its greens and blues.
I am repeating things.
My pen protests. This writing is nonsense, it says.

The world swinging round again, bringing its greens and blues.
Time flaps on the mast—my own phrase.
My pen protests. This writing is nonsense, it says.
But what little I can get down with my pen.

Time flaps on the mast—my own phrase.
Winter has set in. Draw the curtains, light the fire, and so to work.
But what little I can get down with my pen.
I am giving up the hope of being well dressed.

Winter has set in. Draw the curtains, light the fire, and so to work.
Truth is, one can't write about the soul. Looked at, it vanishes.
I am giving up the hope of being well dressed.
One wants to finish sentences.

## Via Negativa

The air in a room after
a door closes. The grotto
of quiet after the last clap.
What occupies a glass when
it's emptied. Two equal parts—
the difference between. The void
housed by a heart squeezed of longing.
The period.        The white after it.
A name on the tip of your tongue.
The earlobe after the earring
is unhung. The no one at the end
of a phone ringing. When a painting
is removed, its cream shadow
unbleached by sun.

# Last

Four days after the funeral
I carry my father's violin
in its long brown box—
sturdy, rectangular, built
to last. In airport security,
its round shoulders glide
through plastic, swallowed
by dark. It emerges
beneath harsh light.

It's September when
I raise the lid, brush dust
from the mute veneer
he touched last spring—
anointing a stuck peg,
sliding rosin on the bow.

I remember the A string
wouldn't tune. He played
anyway. His body leaned
and swayed in its wheelchair
cage. I remember how
the bow strained.

# Sea Psalm

*after Psalm 86*


Let me begin again, Lord.
  For my sins scatter
like starfish at low tide

and my good works are scant.
  Bow the conch ear
of Your kindness, Lord. I am frail

as kelp, flailed on the seabed,
  greedy as the bottom-feeder.
Help me, Lord. Preserve

my soul. When fog breaks
  over the shore, even groundfish
feel the sun. Be merciful.

You possess the patience
  of mollusks. Crack me open.
Make me porous, that Your light

may filter through me like
  the plankton-rich waves.
Your love is boundless as silica,

majestic as the sun. O, bleach
    my blackened bones, Lord.
Grazed and glazed in grit,

even shards become jewels.
    Polish me brighter than nacre.
When pride hardens my heart

into abalone, leave me not
    unturned that in the gleaming
You might see Your face.

## What I Learned This Week

No more fireflies in Northern Indiana.
The fish in Lake Erie are dying out because

they're ingesting plastic microbeads
used in exfoliants. Yellow x's mark

trees on our street that workers will axe
next week. Ash borers are eating them alive

so they cannot absorb water or light. This week I learned
my mother is losing dexterity in both hands.

But when I play Bach-Gounod's *Ave Maria* on the piano, she lifts
her head, motions me to move her wheelchair closer.

She leans over the keyboard to try the melody, finding
the notes each time. Her fingers can barely strike

the keys, but I hear them. Some say music memory
is the last to go. Still, I have no windfalls

for the empty baskets of my mother's eyes.
When I returned from Manila, the peonies I'd left

in half-blossom were stunted by spring storms.
A bud that will not bloom is called a bullet.

# In the Dream I Return Home

*a semi-cento using lines from* Witold Rybczynski's,
*Home: A Short History of an Idea*

I enter my father's room. He leans over his worn table of notes and
pill boxes.

*Personal possessions, a chair, a desk—a place to write. Nothing much
has changed in over four-hundred years.*

In the mirror I watch my mother pinning her dark curls above an
assortment of brushes, powders, and creams.

*Fanny Price had a room where she could go "after anything unpleasant
below."*

I wear my mother's rings. I bake the meatloaf she mixed with bare
fingers. Minced onions sting my eyes.

*To speak of domesticity is to describe a set of felt emotions—not a
single attribute.*

Smell of lightning and rotting wood. In one corner, an overstuffed
chair I read in as a child.

*The appearance of intimacy in the home was the result of another
change taking place in the family: the presence of children.*

The living room empty except for the piano with a broken string.

*Minimal décor has been facetiously described as "conspicuous austerity."*

Opening doors, I search for my father's watch. Behind one door his
   back is turned. This room I do not recognize.

*People turn to the past because they are looking for something they
   cannot find in the present.*

From a hole in the ceiling, purple wires root where a chandelier once hung.

# Self-Portrait as Revision

I am the storm-torn palm frond draped on the balcony wall.
I am the cumin in the soup stirring the lentil's sleep.

I am the olive's skeletal pit, the cat's paw, the thistle spear.
The clay in the kiln cast into a small flask to hold centuries of musk.

For weeks I do not sing, though I gush, an underground rill carving
    blindly to the sea.
I succumb to thunder, the urchin's sting, the softness of moss. This is
    my prayer.

I am driftwood—parched in white heat, soaked in January rain.
A seashell pressed to its pale grave.

The wind rises, rewriting the hymnals of dunes.
I am hurricaned. Worn smooth again.

# NOTES

"Lines from a Journal I" Source text: *Journal of Katherine Mansfield*, edited by J. Middleton Murry. Knopf, 1936.

"September, Chicago" A Golden Shovel poem (a form invented by American poet Terrance Hayes) using a line from Gwendolyn Brooks' poem, "Beverly Hills, Chicago." The line is: "Even the leaves fall down in lovelier patterns here." Each word from this line is an end word in each line of the poem. From Gwendolyn Brooks, *Selected Poems*, Harper Perennial Modern Classics, 2006.

"The Foul Rag and Bone Shop of the Heart" A Golden Shovel poem using a line from William Butler Yeats' poem, "The Circus Animals' Desertion." The line is: "the foul rag and bone shop of the heart." William Butler Yeats, *The Collected Poems of W.B. Yeats*, Scribner, 1996.

"Lines Borrowed from a Marriage and Other Places" The italicized lines, in order of appearance, are from Joyce Carol Oates, Robert Frost, Mary Oliver, and Joan Didion.

> "I never change, I simply become more myself." Joyce Carol Oates, *Solstice: A Novel*, Ontario Review Press, 2000.

> "I shan't be gone long.—You come too." Robert Frost, "The Pasture." *The Poetry of Robert Frost: The Collected Poems*, Complete and Unabridged. Henry Holt, 1979.

"Today again I am hardly myself. It happens over and over." From Mary Oliver, "Reckless Poem." *Five Points Volume VI, Number 3.*

"I've already lost touch with a couple of people I used to be." Joan Didion, *Slouching Towards Bethlehem*, FGSG, 2008.

"The Abscission Layer" The lines in the left column are from an *Encyclopedia Britannica* article on leaf anatomy.

"Lines from a Journal II" Source: *The Diary of Virginia Woolf, Volume 3*. 1925-1930, edited by Anne Olivier Bell. HBJ, 1977. Some of the lines were altered slightly for the purposes of the poem. The original lines are as follows:

"The truth is, one can't write directly about the soul. Looked at, it vanishes."
"To go adventuring on the streams of other people's lives; speculating, adrift."
"Happiness is to have a little string onto which things will attach themselves."
"At this moment, all we wish is to escape seeing anyone."
"The world swinging round again and bringing its green and blue close to one's eyes."
"Time flaps on the mast—my own phrase, I think."
"But what a little I can get down with my pen what is so vivid with my eyes."

"In the Dream I Return Home" The italicized lines are from Witold Rybczynski, *Home: A Short History of an Idea*. Penguin, 1986.

# ACKNOWLEDGMENTS

I am deeply grateful to the editors of the following publications in which these poems first appeared, some of them in slightly different versions or under different titles. *Bellingham Review, Bone Bouquet, Cortland Review, Escape into Life, Green Mountains Review, Jet Fuel Review, Missouri Review, Mom Egg Review, Moria, The Night Heron Barks, [PANK], Pirene's Fountain, POETRY, Poetry South, Quarterly West, Seven Corners, South Florida Poetry Journal, Spoon River Poetry Review, SWWIM, TriQuarterly, Underbelly,* and *Waxwing.*

"Prelude and Fugue," "Narrow Bed," and "Four Years after Diagnosis" were reprinted by *American Academy of Poets.* "Confessions of a Transplant" and "The Immigrant Visits Her Mother" were reprinted in *No Tender Fences: An Anthology of Immigrant & First-Generation American Poetry.* "Four Years after Diagnosis" was reprinted in *Poems for Medical Students* (Keele University School of Medicine, UK). "Feather" was reprinted in *Nevertheless, She Persisted* (Moria Books).

"The Foul Rag and Bone Shop of the Heart" won the 2019 Yeats Poetry Prize awarded by the W.B. Yeats Society of New York and is published on www.yeatssociety.org. "The Immigrant Visits Her Mother" appears in *Puñeta: Political Pilipinx Poetry Vol. 3* (Moria Books). "September, Chicago" appears in *The Golden Shovel Anthology: New Poems Honoring Gwendolyn Brooks* (University of Arkansas Press).

Several poems appear in my chapbook, *To the Bone* (Sundress Publications, 2020).

Endless thanks to my husband Rowie Torres, our sons, Matthew, Ian, and Tim; and Phoebe. Deep gratitude to my poet-sister Naoko Fujimoto. Significant thanks to friends who commented on several poems: Lucía Leao, Yaddyra Peralta, Anthony Madrid, Laura Passin and the December grind group; Gregory Pardlo and his workshop group at the Palm Beach Poetry Festival. My sincere thanks to Martha Rhodes, Ryan Murphy, and Four Way Books.

Angela Narciso Torres is the author of *Blood Orange* (Willow Books Literature Award for Poetry, 2013) and *To the Bone* (Sundress Publications, 2020). Recent work appears in *Poetry, Missouri Review,* and *Quarterly West.* A graduate of Warren Wilson MFA Program for Writers and Harvard Graduate School of Education, Angela has received fellowships from Bread Loaf Writers' Conference, Illinois Arts Council, and Ragdale Foundation. She won the 2019 Yeats Poetry Prize (W.B. Yeats Society of New York) and was named one of *NewCityLit's Lit 50: Who Really Books in Chicago* in 2016. Born in Brooklyn and raised in Manila, she serves as a senior and reviews editor for *RHINO* Poetry. She lives in Southern California.

Publication of this book was made possible by grants and donations. We are also grateful to those individuals who participated in our 2020 Build a Book Program. They are:

Anonymous (14), Robert Abrams, Nancy Allen, Maggie Anderson, Sally Ball, Matt Bell, Laurel Blossom, Adam Bohannon, Lee Briccetti, Therese Broderick, Jane Martha Brox, Christopher Bursk, Liam Callanan, Anthony Cappo, Carla & Steven Carlson, Paul & Brandy Carlson, Renee Carlson, Cyrus Cassells, Robin Rosen Chang, Jaye Chen, Edward W. Clark, Andrea Cohen, Ellen Cosgrove, Peter Coyote, Janet S. Crossen, Kim & David Daniels, Brian Komei Dempster, Matthew DeNichilo, Carl Dennis, Patrick Donnelly, Charles Douthat, Morgan Driscoll, Lynn Emanuel, Monica Ferrell, Elliot Figman, Laura Fjeld, Michael Foran, Jennifer Franklin, Sarah Freligh, Helen Fremont & Donna Thagard, Reginald Gibbons, Jean & Jay Glassman, Ginny Gordon, Lauri Grossman, Naomi Guttman & Jonathan Mead, Mark Halliday, Beth Harrison, Jeffrey Harrison, Page Hill Starzinger, Deming Holleran, Joan Houlihan, Thomas & Autumn Howard, Elizabeth Jackson, Christopher Johanson, Voki Kalfayan, Maeve Kinkead, David Lee, Jen Levitt, Howard Levy, Owen Lewis, Jennifer Litt, Sara London & Dean Albarelli, David Long, James Longenbach, Excelsior Love, Ralph & Mary Ann Lowen, Jacquelyn Malone, Donna Masini, Catherine McArthur, Nathan McClain, Richard McCormick, Victoria McCoy, Ellen McCulloch-Lovell, Judith McGrath, Debbie & Steve Modzelewski, Rajiv Mohabir, James T. F. Moore, Beth Morris, John Murillo & Nicole Sealey, Michael & Nancy Murphy, Maria Nazos, Kimberly Nunes, Bill O'Brien, Susan Okie & Walter Weiss, Rebecca Okrent, Sam Perkins, Megan Pinto, Kyle Potvin, Glen Pourciau, Kevin Prufer, Barbara Ras, Victoria Redel, Martha Rhodes, Paula Rhodes, Paula Ristuccia, George & Nancy Rosenfeld, M. L. Samios, Peter & Jill Schireson, Rob Schlegel, Roni & Richard Schotter, Jane Scovell, Andrew Seligsohn & Martina Anderson, James & Nancy Shalek, Soraya Shalforoosh, Peggy Shinner, Dara-Lyn Shrager, Joan Silber, Emily Sinclair, James Snyder & Krista Fragos, Alice St. Claire-Long, Megan Staffel,

Bonnie Stetson, Yerra Sugarman, Dorothy Tapper Goldman,
Marjorie & Lew Tesser, Earl Teteak, Parker & Phyllis Towle,
Pauline Uchmanowicz, Rosalynde Vas Dias, Connie Voisine, Valerie Wallace,
Doris Warriner, Ellen Doré Watson, Martha Webster & Robert Fuentes,
Calvin Wei, Bill Wenthe, Allison Benis White, Michelle Whittaker, and Ira Zapin.